WAR AND CONFLICT IN THE MIDDLE EAST™

THE INTIFADAS

KATHERINE WINGATE

THE ROSEN PUBLISHING GROUP, INC., NEW YORK

To my family

Published in 2004 by The Rosen Publishing Group, Inc.
29 East 21st Street, New York, NY 10010

Copyright © 2004 by The Rosen Publishing Group, Inc.

First Edition

Library of Congress Cataloging-in-Publication Data

Wingate, Katherine.
The Intifadas / by Katherine Wingate.
    p. cm. — (War and conflict in the Middle East)
Summary: Examines the history behind the intifadas, Palestinian uprisings that were triggered by a traffic accident in 1987, died down, were begun anew in 2000, and are ongoing.
Includes bibliographical references and index.
ISBN 0-8239-4546-4
1. Intifada, 1987—Juvenile literature. [1. Intifada, 1987— 2. Al-Aqsa Intifada, 2000– 3. Palestine—History—20th century.]
I. Title.II. Series.
DS119.75.W56 2003
956.95'3044—dc22

                                                    2003012562

Manufactured in the United States of America

CONTENTS

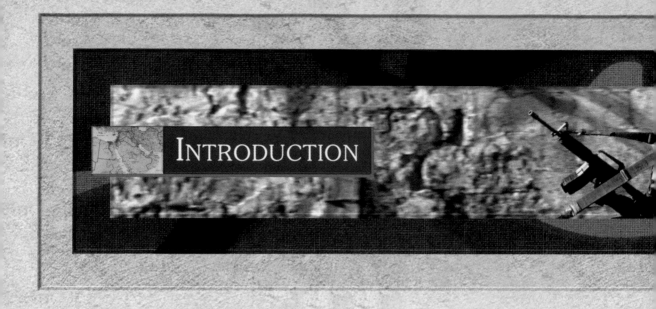

The first intifada issued against Israel began with a traffic accident. On December 8, 1987, an Israeli truck crashed into a car full of Palestinian workers. Four of the workers died, and several more were wounded. The accident happened in Jebalya. Jebalya is the largest Palestinian refugee camp in the Gaza Strip. Its name was taken from a Tel Aviv neighborhood from which many of the refugees fled in 1948.

Traffic accidents are common everywhere; they happened all the time in Jebalya and other cities around the Gaza Strip and Israel itself. Traffic accidents are a fact of life, and no one usually pays much attention to them. This particular incident, however, set off a chain of events no one could ever have predicted.

Soon after news of the accident was broadcast on the radio, rumors started to fly. People said the truck hit the car on purpose. Two days before the accident, an Israeli shopping

at a market in the Gaza Strip was stabbed to death. Palestinians believed that the car crash was an act of revenge for that death. Suddenly, the Palestinians' rage erupted. Like lava from a volcano, it spilled onto the streets of Jebalya. Men, women, and children all took to the streets, riding on a wave of fury. The intifada had begun.

CHAPTER 1

THE UPRISING BEGINS

After the funerals for the victims of the car crash, rioting broke out at the Israeli command post in Jebalya. A small company of officers was stationed there to keep the peace. An angry mob began attacking the compound at dusk. They screamed curses at the officers. They also hurled stones, which were the only weapons they had. This is why the intifada is also known as the War of Stones. "Intifada" itself is an Arabic word that means "to shake off." In political terms, though, it means

"uprising." The Palestinians were rising up against those who they saw were oppressing them: Israel and its military.

A patrol was sent out to disperse the rioters. Some of the concerned officers at the command post approached their section commander. They suggested he call in some reinforcements to help quell the rioting. He remained unconcerned and reassured them that everything would settle down in a short while, It didn't.

The next morning, it became very clear to the fifty-five Israeli officers that this was no ordinary uprising. During the night, the enraged Palestinians had blocked many roads and alleyways with rocks, sewage pipes, and broken furniture. Thousands of people had already taken to the streets. Two armored personnel carriers (APCs) and a Jeep emerged from the compound.

The Israeli military restricts entrance into the Jabalya refugee camp after a shooting incident that left two Israelis dead in August 1987.

They were attempting to break up the roadblocks and show the Palestinians that Israel was still in control. A shower of rocks and stones, angry jeers and curses, and several homemade gasoline bombs (Molotov cocktails) greeted them. Realizing that they were overpowered, the Israeli officers retreated with their APCs back into the compound to regroup. Meanwhile, similar riots had broken out in other refugee camps in the Gaza Strip.

Word of the riots in Gaza spread to Israel's minister of defense, Yitzhak Rabin. Amazingly, he chose to do nothing about it! He too believed the unrest to be another passing phase. On December 10, he instead boarded a plane to the United States. He traveled there to meet with the United States's secretary of defense, Frank Carlucci, to purchase seventy U.S. fighter planes. Because of this and other grave oversights on the part of the Israeli government, the violence spread through Gaza and into the West Bank.

The Young Take Charge

The intifada began as a grassroots movement of the Palestinians living in the occupied territories. They were not organized into any specific political group. In fact they were ordinary people tired of being treated as if they didn't matter. Many felt that their lives were so bad, they had nothing left to lose. It was therefore a social movement and a national uprising.

The majority of these protestors were young people. In 1987, almost half of the population of the West Bank and Gaza Strip was fourteen years of age or younger. Many people

This Land Is Your Land, This Land Is My Land

In the 1800s, European Jews began a movement known as Zionism. It called for the creation of a Jewish homeland in the area known in the Bible as Judea, Israel, Zion, and the Holy Land. Zionists believed that it was impossible to have an authentic Jewish experience while living outside the Holy Land. In 1948, following the end of World War II (1938–1945), the United Nations helped form the State of Israel. However, the many Arabs already living in Palestine felt that their land and identity had been taken away from them. They refused to recognize Israel as a state. They immediately fought against Israel, using the help of surrounding Arab nations. They lost this war and the ability to create their own Palestinian state.

Following the Six-Day War in 1967, Israel took control of vast areas of land densely populated by Arabs. These areas are known as the occupied territories. They include the West Bank and Gaza Strip. Today, the combined Arab population in these territories totals approximately 3.5 million people.

In the occupied territories, refugee camps were formed to house the Palestinians whose land had been taken from them. Conditions in the occupied territories and refugee camps were harsh. The Palestinians had very few rights. For instance, one could be jailed for voicing one's political opinion, especially if it criticized Israeli rule. Israel often even blew up the houses of known or suspected dissenters. To Israel, this was simply a matter of national security. After the horrors of the Holocaust, Israeli Jews felt compelled to protect their rights and their property, even if it meant restricting the rights of Palestinians living in the occupied territories. Israelis felt they had done all they could to reach a compromise with the Palestinians. In 1987, after twenty years of Israeli control, the Palestinians living in the West Bank and Gaza Strip rose up in rebellion. This rebellion became known as the intifada.

were able to send their children off to schools and universities. At school, many of them became politically active and joined student groups associated with different factions of the Palestine Liberation Organization (PLO). They organized demonstrations and strikes to protest the Israeli occupation.

These youths and their families suffered because they were subject to harassment on a daily basis. The young people were also disillusioned with the older generation's inability to

Israeli Arabs in support of the uprisings in Gaza and the West Bank participated in a sympathy strike in Nazareth on December 21, 1987. Shown above, an armed Israeli Jew wearing a gas mask corners an Arab rioter in the street.

do anything against the Israeli occupation. So when the intifada began, the young were the people who fueled its fire.

The Uprising Expands

Outside of Gaza, the intifada took on a new life. What started as a spontaneous expression of Palestinian rage became an intentional uprising. People began to organize and plot the course of the revolt to make sure that it did not die out. In Jerusalem, two brothers named Mohammed and Majid Labadi saw the potential of the intifada and decided to act. They wanted to carry out a plan that would set this uprising apart from previous ones and boost its momentum. They brought in about forty volunteers from Gaza and Hebron to help them carry out their plan.

On December 19 at precisely 9:20 AM, riots broke out all across Jerusalem. The rioters put up barricades of burning tires, ransacked Israeli-owned businesses, and took part in violent demonstrations. The plan worked. Over 5,000 of Jerusalem's Arabs joined the struggle against the Israeli occupation.

This time, however, Israel hastily sent reinforcements to combat the protestors. More than 1,000 policemen were brought in to help put a stop to the riots. For the most part, they used means other than direct force to stop the Palestinians taking part in the uprising. The Israeli police made life very difficult for the protestors. They imposed strict curfews on whole villages and performed random searches of people and vehicles. Israel hoped that these harsher conditions would stop the rebellion, but instead they did the opposite.

CHAPTER 2

WHO'S IN CONTROL HERE?

As the uprising spread to Jerusalem and beyond, the Palestinian commoners who started the rebellion began to organize. They felt an ownership of the uprising, but so did Yasser Arafat. Arafat was the leader of the PLO, a group devoted to achieving Palestinian independence from Israel. He quickly tried to take control of the situation. He wanted people to believe that the uprising was started as a political move, not as a result of Palestinian anger. What resulted was a handful of different command organizations, all trying to take the lead and plot the course of the intifada.

The Unified National Command

In late December 1987, the Palestinians founded an organization to lead the intifada. They called it the Unified National Command (UNC). At the beginning, however, the UNC was anything but unified. Even though all the organizations in the UNC were fighting for the liberation of Palestine, each had a different idea of how to get there. As a result, they were often very suspicious and distrustful of each other.

The UNC assumed leadership of the uprising and directed the actions of those participating in it. It was made up of four different factions of the PLO: the Democratic

Masking his identity, a Palestinian carrying a stone wanders through the rubble in the West Bank. Because the intifada was a civilian uprising, makeshift weapons such as stones were used in combat.

Yasser Arafat

Yasser Arafat is a man who wears a hundred faces. Sometimes he appears kind and caring, while at other times he can be ruthless and cold-hearted. Many hate him and many love him. Few, however, can call up an image of the Palestinian-Israeli conflict and not see his face. This is with good reason: Arafat has dedicated his life to the Palestinian struggle for independence. Even as a teenager in the 1940s, Arafat fought against the British occupation of Jerusalem. Following the creation of the State of Israel, in 1964 he and a few of his friends founded an organization called Fatah.

Yasser Arafat, 1987

Fatah called for armed resistance to Israeli rule and the creation of a Palestinian state. Fatah quickly became the strongest and most influential group in the Palestine Liberation Organization. In 1969, Fatah took over the PLO, and Yasser Arafat became its chairman. Arafat set up the PLO's permanent headquarters in various places, such as Jordan, Lebanon, Tunis, and Egypt, because he was exiled from Israel at the time. Arafat was forced to leave most of these places because of the turmoil the PLO caused each time it set up offices and a military presence.

Front for the Liberation of Palestine (DFLP), Fatah, the Popular Front for the Liberation of Palestine (PFLP), and the Palestine Communist Party (PCP). Each had one representative in the UNC. Regardless of the size of their followings, they agreed to share an equal status with each other.

Yasser Arafat complicated matters by refusing to recognize the Unified National Command as anything but an "arm" of the PLO. Even though he had no direct part in starting the uprising, he felt entitled to the true command of the intifada. This angered the members of the UNC because they considered themselves better representatives of the uprising than Arafat. However, the UNC agreed to remain within the existing PLO network so it could keep the support of the leadership in Tunis.

To truly lead the uprising, the Unified National Command had to take its message to the streets. The best way it found to do this was through distributing handbills, or leaflets. In early January 1988, the still-forming UNC issued its first handbill. In it, the UNC called for a three-day general strike in the territories. It also listed a number of demands. The UNC wanted the Israeli army to fully withdraw from the occupied territories. It also demanded a halt to the building of new Jewish settlements in the territories. Finally, it called for democratic elections to be held in the West Bank and Gaza Strip. Ultimately, the handbill stated, its goal was the formation of a Palestinian state.

The Israel Defense Force

The IDF is Israel's military. Its mission is to defend the State of Israel and its inhabitants. The IDF is made up of a small standing army, an air force, and a navy. Its main tasks include enforcing the peace arrangements between Israel and the Palestinians and guarding against terrorism. Every Israeli citizen upon reaching the age of eighteen is expected to serve in the IDF in some form. Women serve for two years. Men serve for three years, followed by a period of service in the reserve army.

Israel Strikes Back

Meanwhile, Israel was struggling with how to control and ultimately stop the rebellion. Israel's army generals didn't want to stop the uprising through military force alone. But others argued that the only way to quell the uprising was through force. They believed that the Israel Defense Force (IDF) was being too soft on the rioting Palestinians.

Finally, in mid-January, the IDF struck back. It deployed two brigades to the West Bank and one to the Gaza Strip. Thousands of Israeli soldiers were now stationed in the territories to restore order and keep the peace. However, they found themselves in the middle of a debate on how they should respond to the violent protestors. Many politicians suggested they use an "iron fist" and respond with violence. Most soldiers and army generals, however, didn't want to risk harming innocent bystanders. They favored less harsh punishments like

Israeli soldiers drag a Palestinian prisoner down the street. Soldiers were reluctant to use violence to control the Palestinians but felt it was the only way to contain the fury of the Palestinian rebellion.

imposing village curfews and cutting off villages' telephone and electricity lines.

As the intifada escalated, however, Israeli defense minister Yitzhak Rabin ordered his troops to respond more directly. For instance, they were told to shoot any person who threw a Molotov cocktail. They were also ordered to demolish some protestors' homes. Many times

In this photo taken in 1988, the Israeli defense minister, Yitzhak Rabin, meets with soldiers in Ramallah, West Bank, to discuss military plans. Rabin also served as prime minister from 1974 to 1977 and again in 1992 until he was assassinated by a fundamentalist Jewish student in 1995.

the protestor's family was close by, overcome with sadness and rage. Even though these extreme punishments added to the Palestinians' fury, it reduced their use of Molotov cocktails.

Later, Rabin distributed clubs to IDF soldiers and ordered them to beat anyone defying Israeli law. He thought this approach was more humane than resorting to firearms and more acceptable to the soldiers, the Palestinians, and the world community. He couldn't have been more wrong, though. Graphic footage of Israeli soldiers beating Palestinian men, women, and children was broadcast around the world. This caused an outpouring of criticism from all sides. Some Israeli Jews even spoke out against such harsh treatment. Many IDF soldiers were also opposed to this method but had to follow their orders. They knew that the people they were clubbing were humans just like themselves and didn't deserve such inhumane treatment.

Soon, Israeli settlers in the occupied territories found themselves in harm's way because of the violence all around them. They blamed the IDF for failing to provide them with adequate protection. Sometimes in anger they even blocked roads and held protests similar to those of the Palestinians! The intifada showed these settlers that, like it or not, they were living in a battleground.

CHAPTER 3

ARE YOU WITH US OR AGAINST US?

During the second month of the intifada, a group called Hamas (meaning "zeal" in Arabic) took the stage. Hamas was a religious organization that favored a return to traditional Islamic lifestyle. It lashed out not only at Israelis, but also at Palestinian "collaborators" with Israel. The intifada had taken yet another turn: now the enemy wasn't only on the outside, but inside, as well.

Hamas Gains Support

A young member of Hamas uses a slingshot to shoot at Israeli soldiers during a protest against the peace talks. Hamas states that its mission is to destroy the nation of Israel.

To gain support, Hamas issued handbills similar to those of the UNC. It also called for general strikes. Although Hamas refused to join the UNC, it never tried to undermine it either. Rather, Hamas sought to draw as many Palestinians as it could into Islam. Hamas's following grew considerably in the first few months of the uprising, causing Israel to take serious notice. What made Hamas members especially threatening to Israeli national security was the fact that they were willing to die for their cause.

Soon Hamas members started stockpiling weapons to use against Israelis. They didn't want to limit themselves to throwing stones like the rest of the protestors. When the Israelis caught wind of this armed underground, they swooped down and arrested more than a hundred Hamas members. This severely weakened Hamas but didn't destroy it. Rather, the movement eventually recovered and grew in strength. Israelis sent the Palestinians they arrested to detention camps and prisons. Even though they were imprisoned, they stayed involved with Hamas. When prisoners' families came to visit, they passed secret notes. Sometimes family members even passed notes to the prisoners while kissing them. The prisoners then kept the notes in their mouths and read them when they were back safely in their cells.

Popular Committees

When the intifada began, most Palestinians were so caught up in the moment that they didn't even consider their next step. But after two months of mass protests, stone throwing, and barricades, they had to consider the movement's future. Now that they had set the wheels in motion, where were they trying to go, and how would they get there?

A man named Mubarak Awad encouraged Palestinians to stage nonviolent protests. This is also known as civil disobedience. Awad envisioned a completely self-sufficient Palestinian state that didn't rely on Israel for anything. Within this Palestinian state, there would be separate committees to take care of things like health care and education. He suggested more than a hundred ways to achieve this vision. These included refusing to pay fines to Israel, refusing to work in Israeli factories, and violating curfews imposed by Israel.

Friend Against Friend

Popular committees weren't the only ways Palestinians got organized. Early in the uprising, gangs of thugs terrorized the Palestinian public. They were called shock forces. The shock forces lashed out at Israelis, but also at fellow Palestinians. They targeted Palestinians who were known or suspected collaborators with Israel. Collaborators were basically spies for Israel. They gave the Israelis inside information about the intifada. Shock forces often brutally beat or killed the spies, and sometimes they burned down their houses.

Things began to spiral out of control. More and more people were punished for collaborating with Israel. Many of them were innocent, so the image of the movement was hurt. Palestinians lived in terror of being accused and killed. Soon, shock forces attacked people for moral reasons as well. Drug dealers and prostitutes, among others, were singled out for "immoral behavior." These attacks were geared toward the "purification of society." Often, Hamas was behind these attacks. Even though the UNC condemned all retaliations, the attacks continued.

The Unified National Command soon took notice of Awad's ideas. Suddenly, his vision of a free Palestine showed up in UNC handbills. The Palestinians decided that they didn't just want an end to the Israeli occupation. They wanted to re-create the homeland they felt Israel took from them.

Awad's vision of independent committees soon took hold throughout the territories. Common people who hadn't been able to participate in the intifada poured their energy into these "popular committees." There were committees to take care of the families of the dead or wounded, to distribute food to the needy, and to provide health care to the Palestinians. Agricultural committees advocated farming on abandoned or vacant lots. They also taught people how to raise chickens and rabbits at home. The UNC endorsed and encouraged the growth of popular committees. The fruits of their labor brought Palestinians one step closer to self-sufficiency.

Some Palestinians argued that there was still a need for violent acts to keep the uprising going strong. Soon, protests turned violent again. Israel responded in the summer of 1988 by shutting down the majority of popular committees. That meant only the most violent protestors remained. Many of them went into hiding to escape arrest.

Stalemate

Late in 1988, Israel again cracked down on Palestinian protestors. Israel built new prisons and detention centers and arrested hundreds of people. It limited Palestinian mobility with mass curfews and military roadblocks. Israeli authorities cut off the water, electricity, and phone lines in many villages as well. As a result, many people were unable to transport their goods to market. The Palestinian standard of living fell by between 30 and 40 percent. Israel's economy suffered as well. Because of the uprising, Israel lost more than $1 billion in expected revenue. Hit with such hard times, Palestinians fell back to lick their wounds.

The intifada was slowly wearing away at both sides in the conflict. The leaders of the intifada were low on funds. Because of this, they were unable to keep the uprising as

The Gaza Strip is home to 4,000 Jewish settlers and more than one million Palestinians. Israel took control of the area during the Arab-Israeli War (1948–49). Above, a Palestinian woman surveys the destruction in the Gaza Strip in 1988.

large scale as it had been at the beginning of the intifada. Israel was weakened as well. Despite its state-of-the-art weaponry, Israel had lost much of its self-confidence. Israelis could no longer pretend that things would ever go back to "normal." But neither side was willing to give up.

Palestinians Declare Independence

Late in the day on July 31, 1988, Israeli officials raided an office in a research institute called the Society for Arab Studies. They confiscated a document called "Plan for Making a Declaration of Independence." The document was written by a key leader of the Fatah organization. Contained in the document was an extensive plan outlining the partitioning of Israel into separate Israeli and Palestinian states. After reading the document, Israel made it clear that it would take whatever means necessary to prevent the Palestinians from declaring independence. However, Israeli authorities were unable to stop the inevitable. Also on that date, Jordan renounced its claim to the West Bank. It conceded that only the PLO represented Palestinians.

When the Palestine National Council (PNC) met on November 15, 1988, the overwhelming majority voted in favor of declaring Palestinian independence from the State of Israel. The members also voted in favor of having an international conference for peace in the Middle East. In doing so, the Palestinians made a definitive statement to Israel and the rest of the world—they were ready to negotiate. They also recognized Israel's right to exist. This was a pioneering move!

Palestinian supporters rally against the Israeli supporters in Strasbourg, France, in 1988. Yasser Arafat visited the European Parliament to affirm Palestine's commitment to peaceful negotiations, but he still refused to recognize the State of Israel.

Now that Palestinians had declared independence, they had to be able to support the population without Israeli assistance. Popular committees laid the framework for health care, school, and agricultural systems. The IDF responded by doing anything possible to disrupt these planning sessions. Israel wanted to prevent the Arabs from putting their plans into action. They knew that by getting organized, the Palestinians would be more determined than ever.

Conflicts between Jews and Arabs raged on while world leaders sat down to talks aimed at ending the intifada. While some of the Jewish population saw the end of the intifada as a step toward peace, others felt the negotiations made Israel vulnerable to further attacks.

Israel's Reaction

Some Jews supported the Palestinians' move toward statehood. They were just as tired of all the fighting as the Arabs. They agreed that the Palestinians had every right to a separate state. Some Israelis helped peace and human rights organizations in the occupied territories. They proved that not all Jews agreed with the occupation of Palestinian territory.

However, many Israelis reacted with much less compassion. They were angry with the Palestinians, but they were also angry with their own government for lying to them. Israeli officials had told them that the Palestinians were better off now that they were under Israeli rule. They even said that the Palestinian people weren't really Palestinians anymore, but Israelis! Instead, Jews found themselves confronted by a people who very much did exist. They were also faced with the possibility of violence every time they stepped out their front door. Needless to say, this made many Jews furious with their elected officials and with the press for covering up the truth.

These Israelis accused their media of distorting the news and supporting the uprising. Some Jewish settlers in the occupied territories even attacked news reporters and pollsters whose reports were upsetting to them. Racism became more common. In one Israeli town, there was talk of closing a school attended by both Jewish and Arab children. Some rabbis even spoke in favor of killing Arabs. Clearly, Israelis still had a long way to go before they could live in peace with the Palestinians.

CHAPTER 4

ON THE ROAD TO STATEHOOD

It was into this atmosphere of continued conflict that George Schultz, the United States secretary of state, entered. He had been working with the Arabs and Israelis for a long time, trying to help them make peace with each other. Because of the stubbornness he encountered on both sides, he failed time and time again. He wanted nothing more than to just get out and leave it all up to them. However, when the intifada broke out, Schultz once again found himself back in the thick of it.

Schultz Steps In

The United States has been a close ally and supporter of Israel for decades. Because of this, the United States had refused to work directly with the PLO. However, Israel's prime minister, Yitzhak Shamir, was unwilling to deal with the PLO as well. He told Schultz that he was firmly opposed to the creation of a Palestinian state. Schultz realized that he was getting nowhere with Shamir. In a bold and unprecedented move, Schultz opened negotiations with the PLO soon after it declared independence from Israel and recognized its right to exist.

Talking Peace with the PLO

George Schultz's decision to talk with the PLO paid off. He urged Yasser Arafat to

U.S. secretary of state George Schultz *(left)* meets with Lieutenant General Colin Powell, Howard Baker, and President Reagan in the Oval Office to discuss how they will negotiate with the PLO.

Yitzhak Shamir

Yitzhak Shamir was involved with Israeli politics from the country's first days. In his twenties, Shamir led a small militant group called Fighters for the Freedom of Israel (known as the Stern Gang). Shamir was arrested twice because of his extreme views and activism. He managed to escape both times. He continued his political career, holding positions as speaker of the Israeli Parliament and as foreign minister. In 1983 he was elected prime minister. He served in that position for more than seven years. While in office, Shamir was responsible for the immigration of a million Jews to Israel. These immigrants came mostly from the Soviet Union. This immigration policy earned him a bad reputation among Palestinians. They felt he was trying to squeeze them out of what little land they had left. Shamir was defeated in the 1992 election, and in 1996 he retired from the political scene.

Yitzhak Shamir, 1983

publicly renounce terrorism. In return, Schultz promised, the United States would openly enter into a dialogue with the PLO. Arafat accepted these terms. On December 14, 1988, he renounced terrorism in front of the United Nations General Assembly. The United States made good on its word. America made public its decision to work directly with Arafat and the PLO.

When Shamir found out the United States had opened talks with the PLO, he contacted President Ronald Reagan to protest. This time, though, Shamir was too late. He'd had his chance to cooperate on the peace process. Now the United States and PLO were moving ahead whether he liked it or not. Like Shamir, some Israelis resisted the winds of change that were sweeping over the Middle East. Others quickly recovered from their shock over the United States's decision and tried to adapt to the new political terrain. With Reagan's term ending and George H. W. Bush's beginning, the American players were switching faces. A new U.S. secretary of state, James Baker, was soon to be appointed. At this crucial time, all sides wondered how this change would affect the peace process. The PLO seemed to be offering an olive branch, but would Israel accept it?

Back in the USSR

By 1989, the intifada was in its second year. What began as a conflict between two groups was now a major world issue. It drew other countries into the fray. These countries were like players in a giant game of chess. Before making their next move, each tried to calculate how the others would react. The United States recognized the PLO. The PLO offered to work with Israel. Now another major player, the Soviet Union, made its move.

In the past, the Soviet Union had refused to have diplomatic relations with Israel. It chose to work with the Arab states instead. It had even supplied mass weaponry to some Arab countries such as Syria and Egypt. Now that tensions were mounting in the Middle East, the Soviets feared that Syria might use some of these weapons against Israel. The Soviets didn't want to be blamed if that happened, so they offered to work with both sides to help them achieve peace.

Israel viewed the Soviets' extended hand with suspicion. After all, hadn't the Soviets supported all of Israel's enemies in the past? Why should Israelis trust them now? In the end, however, Israel did choose to accept the Soviet Union's support. It hoped the Soviets would continue to restrain Syria and the other Arab regimes opposed to peace.

Shamir's Plan

After America opened talks with the Palestinians, Shamir's advisors urged him to act fast. Television images of Israeli brutality against Palestinians aired across the world daily. Many nations started to wonder if Israel was willing to do anything to stop the violent intifada. Israel was quickly losing ground. It had to show the world community that it was still willing to negotiate on the Palestinian issue.

In response, Shamir crafted a peace initiative. His plan called for elections to be held in the occupied territories. The elected representatives were to work with Israel to negotiate a five-year period of autonomy, or self-rule. His plan stated that within three years, both sides would begin negotiations for a permanent solution. However, he was still solidly opposed to Palestinian statehood and still refused to talk directly with the PLO.

Many innocent lives were lost during the intifada. One of the first victims was a young Palestinian schoolgirl who was shot in the back by an Israeli soldier. Above, a Palestinian woman weeps at the grave of her fifteen-year-old child.

The Palestinians rejected Shamir's plan because it excluded the PLO. Furthermore, the PLO and the UNC called for continued violence against Israelis and Palestinian collaborators with Israel. The intifada's leaders called on Palestinians to kill one Israeli soldier for every Palestinian killed by Israeli troops. This certainly didn't strengthen Israel's trust in them. The Palestinians' credibility was further flawed when the Gulf War began in 1991. The PLO was one

On December 8, 1990, Arab leaders met in Baghdad to discuss Palestine. *From left to right:* The vice president of Yemen, Ali Salem Al Beedh; King Hussein of Jordan; Iraqi president Saddam Hussein; and Palestinian leader Yasser Arafat.

of Saddam Hussein's biggest supporters. During the war, Hussein heavily bombed Israel. This made Israel wonder if the Palestinians' desire for peace was just a charade.

The Madrid Conference

When the Palestinians declared independence, they called for an international peace conference. United States secretary of state James Baker helped make this dream a reality. During the summer of 1991, Baker made several trips to the Middle East to invite nations there to participate in the conference. There were two main goals of the conference. One was to help bring about talks between Israel and its Arab neighbors. The other was to reach a peaceful solution to the Palestinian-Israeli conflict. Prime Minister Shamir grudgingly agreed to participate. He held firm on his conviction not to speak with the PLO leadership. Again, he made it clear that he was opposed to the formation of a Palestinian state.

From October 30 through November 1, 1991, Israel, Syria, Lebanon, Jordan, and the Palestinians met in Madrid, Spain. Surprisingly, Shamir left open the door for a territorial compromise with the Palestinians. The Arab response was less restrained. With the flames of the intifada fueling him, the Palestinian representative, Haider Abdel-Shafi, demanded Palestinian sovereignty in less than five years. The conference ended without any resolution. Everyone agreed they should meet again, though. It was an achievement for Palestinians and Israelis simply to sit together at the negotiating table. Slowly, they were inching their way to a compromise.

CHAPTER 5

THE END OR JUST THE BEGINNING?

eanwhile, Shamir had other things to think about. In his 1983 inaugural speech, he had vowed to continue to build Jewish settlements in the occupied territories. He went so far as to call it his "holy work." In the late 1980s, he got his chance.

Israel Opens Its Doors

After the collapse of the Soviet Union, many Russian Jews looked to Israel as a new homeland. Between 1989 and 1991,

masses of Russian Jews immigrated to Israel. All in all, within a decade, more than one million people left the former Soviet Union for Israel. On top of that, war and chaos broke out in Ethiopia in early 1991. Thousands of Ethiopian Jews were stranded in the crossfire. Shamir orchestrated a dramatic air rescue, called Operation Solomon. He brought 14,324 of the Ethiopian Jews to Israel to resettle.

To accommodate this great influx of people, Shamir asked the United States for a loan. In 1990, the United States granted Israel $400 million to help build settlements for the new immigrant Jews. However, as more and more immigrants poured into Israel, Shamir saw he needed more money to house them. He asked President Bush for an additional $10 billion. This time his

In May 1991, the Ethiopian People's Revolutionary Democratic Front took hold of the Ethiopian government and sent totalitarian ruler Mengistu Haile Mariam into exile. Pictured here is a blind Ethiopian woman being carried off an airplane.

request was denied. President Bush knew that Shamir's aggressive settlement plan was getting in the way of the peace process. It seemed more and more evident that peace was the last thing on Shamir's mind.

Enter Rabin

In June 1992, the Israeli electorate voted Shamir out of power. They knew that peace was impossible to achieve with him in office. In his place, they appointed Yitzhak Rabin as prime minister. With Shamir out of the picture, people on both sides of the conflict felt renewed optimism.

It looked like peace might be on the horizon. Then, terror struck in the United States. On February 26, 1993, Islamic terrorists planted a truck bomb in the garage beneath the World Trade Center in New York City. Dozens of people were wounded in the explosion, and six were killed. The men who carried out the attack were angry that the United States was still supporting Israel. They also felt that Western culture was to blame for cracks in the foundation of their Islamic faith. Many people feared that extremists such as these men would undermine the peace process, but they were wrong. Behind the scenes, Israel and the PLO had begun negotiating in secret.

The Oslo Peace Accords

The news began to leak out in the summer of 1993. Top-level officials from both Israel and the PLO were secretly working together in Oslo, Norway. In fact, they'd been meeting for

Yitzhak Rabin

Yitzhak Rabin was, above all, a military man. He received his first military training at age thirteen and grew up with the IDF. Rabin went on to lead the Israeli army to victory in the Six-Day War. His time in the army prepared him well for his political career. He learned to be straightforward, disciplined, and direct, and he always maintained a stiff upper lip. He never showed any doubt or weakness. These qualities helped him attain the position of

Yitzhak Rabin, 1993

prime minister in 1974. He was the first prime minister born and raised in Israel. During his time in office, he worked to strengthen the IDF and Israel's economy. In 1977, he resigned his position due to a scandal. He and his wife were discovered to have an illegal bank account in the United States. He fell back into the shadows and bided his time. In the 1980s, Rabin reemerged into the political spotlight. He served as minister of defense during the first intifada, from 1984 to 1990. In 1992, Rabin was again elected prime minister. After signing the Declaration of Principles, he and Yasser Arafat were awarded the Nobel Peace Prize. Rabin was assassinated at a peace rally on November 4, 1995. His killer was a fellow Jew who disagreed with Rabin's policies. Rabin was seventy-three when he died. Despite his cold demeanor, he helped bring Israel one step closer to peace with the Palestinians.

months. Norway was the staging point for these talks because it was friendly with both sides and thus neutral. Officials attending the talks took pains to remain undetected. For instance, they flew to different airports and stayed in different hotels. They worried that if the negotiations were made public, they might not make as much progress. The United States, now under the administration of President Bill Clinton, was aware that the talks were being held. Beyond that, all credit for the progress belonged to Israel and the PLO.

U.S. president Bill Clinton brings Israeli prime minister Yitzhak Rabin and PLO chairman Yasser Arafat together for a famous handshake. The Oslo Accords was the first agreement between Israelis and Palestinians expressing a mutual wish to end the fighting and share the land.

The secret talks were successful. On September 13, 1993, Yitzhak Rabin and Yasser Arafat signed the Israeli-Palestinian Declaration of Principles, also known as the Oslo Accords. The whole world watched as these two men, bitter enemies for years, shook hands. And with that handshake, the intifada came to a close after almost six years of fighting.

Under the Oslo Accords, Israel and the PLO recognized each other and laid out the terms for Palestinian self-rule. They agreed that Gaza and Jericho would be the first areas Israel would hand over to the Palestinians. The rest of the territories were to follow shortly. Israel gave the Palestinians full responsibility for social services such as health care, education, and welfare. In return, the PLO again renounced terrorism and acknowledged Israel's right to exist. Israeli citizens were allowed to remain in the West Bank and Gaza Strip. Israel retained control over the bridges into Jordan and remained in charge of security throughout the territories. They put off any final decision on who would control the hotly contested area of Jerusalem.

Happily Ever After?

Unfortunately, the peace agreement had no fairy-tale ending. The Declaration of Principles was a major step on the road to peace, but old wounds still flared on both sides. Just because Rabin and Arafat shook hands didn't mean that ordinary Israelis and Palestinians would do the same. Both the Popular Front for the Liberation of Palestine and the Democratic Front for the Liberation of Palestine rejected

Protests still abound, though many pains were taken to find peaceful solutions to the Palestinian-Israeli conflict. Many Israelis were infuriated by the idea of recognizing a Palestinian state, while many Palestinians felt the same way about an Israeli state.

the Oslo Accords. They suspended their participation in the PLO as a result. Hamas refused to honor the agreement. Also refusing was the Islamic Jihad, another militant Islamic group determined to destroy Israel simply through holy war. All these factions vowed to continue campaigns of violence against Israelis. Their only goal was the liberation of all of Palestine, not just parts of it.

In many ways the Declaration of Principles was a solution based on convenience. Israel knew it was the best deal it could get at the time, while the PLO was fast running out of funding. Building a peace agreement without the full support of their people was risky. However, it was a risk both sides felt they had to take. Only time would tell if this "peace" could last.

CHAPTER 6

THE INTIFADA, PART TWO

On Thursday, September 28, 2000, Israeli politician Ariel Sharon visited a holy site for both Jews and Muslims in Jerusalem called the Noble Sanctuary on Mount Temple. Housed within this compound is the Al-Aqsa Mosque. Each Friday, thousands of Muslim worshipers gather there to pray. Sharon's visit to the mosque angered the Palestinians there. They knew he was trying to assert Israel's right to the Noble Sanctuary. Infuriated, they began to riot. Sharon's armed escorts fired back at the protestors with rubber bullets. Four unarmed Palestinians were killed during this outbreak of violence, and over 200 were wounded. The protests quickly spread through the Gaza Strip and the West Bank. A new Palestinian intifada had begun. It became known as the Al-Aqsa intifada. It has continued right up to the present day.

From the beginning, the Al-Aqsa intifada has been more violent than the first uprising. Because of a decade of failed peace initiatives, tensions among Israelis and Palestinians are higher than ever before. Many Palestinian protestors have traded in their stones for rifles and bombs. Israel has moved from using clubs and rubber bullets to F-16 jets and tanks. Instead of bringing about peace, the violence only seems to create more violence. To date,

Right-wing opposition leader Ariel Sharon (center) stands outside of the Al-Aqsa Mosque surrounded by his security guards.

Israeli policemen lead a bleeding Palestinian man away from an area where stone-throwing youths challenged the police. Many incidents such as this occurred in the West Bank and Gaza, hotbeds of social unrest during the intifadas.

2,298 Palestinians and 787 Israelis have been killed since September 2000. Sadly, these numbers grow every day.

From Oslo to Al-Aqsa

The Oslo Accords might have ended the first intifada, but they didn't stop Palestinian-Israeli violence. Things looked good at the beginning, though. In 1994, Israel began to withdraw its forces from Gaza and the West Bank. It also helped the Palestinians to create their own interim government, called the Palestinian Authority (PA). Yasser Arafat returned to Gaza after twenty-seven years of exile and was eventually elected president of the PA.

In the years that followed, however, Israel became angry with the Palestinians because they weren't following through on promises they'd made. Palestinians had agreed to crack down on acts of terrorism against Israel. They also pledged to amend their charter, which still called for the destruction of the State of Israel. Arafat and the Palestinian Authority refused to comply on these issues, even though they signed several more peace agreements saying they would. As a result, Israel stopped moving its troops out of the occupied territories.

The United States and several other countries tried to help Palestinians and Israelis get back on track but were unsuccessful. In July 2000, President Clinton met with Yasser Arafat and Israeli prime minister Ehud Barak at Camp David, the United States presidential retreat in Maryland. There, Barak offered Arafat a better settlement deal than Israel had ever offered before. Arafat refused the offer flat-out and didn't even suggest an alternative solution. He simply walked out, leaving nothing left of the Oslo Accords but empty words and broken promises. Several weeks later, the Al-Aqsa intifada erupted in Jerusalem. This placed the final nail in the coffin that was the Israeli-Palestinian peace process.

Why Another Intifada?

The Al-Aqsa intifada started because the Palestinian people were still not satisfied with Israel's peace offerings. They wanted Israel to return all of East Jerusalem, not just parts of it. They also wanted the one thing Israel swore they could never have: the right for all Palestinian refugees since 1948 to return to their homeland. To Israel, that demand amounted to the destruction of the Jewish state. Ariel Sharon's visit to the Noble Sanctuary only sparked the fuse that resulted in the uprising. In fact, the second intifada had been planned in advance. Palestinians had begun planning it right after Arafat walked out of the Camp David summit earlier in 2000. They didn't know what event would start it off, but they knew it was on the horizon.

Two Years and Counting

Early in 2001, the Palestinians adopted a new tactic—suicide bombings. Palestinians from groups like Hamas often carry out these deadly attacks. Suicide bombers willingly blow themselves up in order to become martyrs and kill Jews. Their religious

Ariel Sharon

Ariel Sharon is not easily pushed around. In 1953, he founded and led a secret Israeli commando unit called Unit 101. Its job was to seek out and destroy the bases of Palestinian terrorists. He then went on to an impressive military career. He commanded armored divisions in the 1967 Six-Day War as well as in the 1973 Yom Kippur War. In 1981, Sharon was appointed defense minister. While serving in that position, he authorized Israel's invasion of Lebanon to break up the PLO's infrastructure there. Thousands of innocent civilians were killed or wounded in that campaign. Throughout the 1990s,

Ariel Sharon, 2001

Sharon ushered in massive numbers of immigrants and provided them with housing, often in the occupied territories. He was elected prime minister on February 6, 2001. This was only four months after his fateful visit to the Noble Sanctuary, which set off the Al-Aqsa intifada. Under Sharon's leadership, Israel has been accused of numerous human rights violations concerning its harsh treatment of Palestinian demonstrators.

leaders tell them that if they die fighting for their freedom, they will be rewarded in heaven. Suicide bombers often detonate the bombs in areas crowded with many Israelis. Their intent is to cause as many Israeli casualties as possible. Since the intifada began, there have been countless suicide attacks on Israeli soldiers and civilians. Hundreds of people have died as a result.

On March 27, 2002, a suicide bomber blew himself up in the lobby of a hotel in central Israel. Hundreds of Jews had gathered there to celebrate the first night of Passover.

A press photographer looks over the damage done to a Netanya, Israel hotel after a suicide bombing on March 27, 2002. Nineteen people were killed and 140 were wounded in the unexpected attack.

At least nineteen people were killed, and more than 100 others were wounded. This attack became known in Israel as the Passover massacre. This horrendous attack caused Israel to launch Operation Defensive Shield on March 29. The IDF called up more than 20,000 reserve soldiers. They systematically reoccupied most of the cities under the control of the Palestinian Authority. In Ramallah, they took over the presidential compound where Arafat lived. Israel held him hostage there without electricity, water, or phone lines. Ariel Sharon declared that Israel was at war.

During Operation Defensive Shield, Palestinian towns and cities were placed under extensive curfews. Residents were confined to their homes for weeks. No one from the outside was allowed to enter the area. This caused massive shortages of food, water, and medical supplies. Many Palestinians were shot if they simply went outside. Others died because they were unable to go to the hospital to receive medical care. The United States strongly pressured Sharon to pull troops out of the Palestinian areas in order to stop the killing going on there. By April 21, Israel had withdrawn from all but two of the areas it had reoccupied. On May 1, Israel ended the monthlong siege on Arafat's compound.

The Roadmap for Peace

In the spring of 2002, the United States formed a coalition with the United Nations, Russia, and the European Union. This coalition is called the Quartet. They got together to draft a new plan for peace between Israel and the Palestinians. The Quartet said it would present the peace plan only if the Palestinian Authority appointed a prime minister. The United States believed that Yasser Arafat hadn't offered the kind of leadership necessary for bringing about peace. The Palestinians agreed to the United States's request. On April 23, 2003, a man named Mahmud Abbas was appointed Palestinian prime minister. He had played an important role in drafting the Oslo Accords in 1993. President George W. Bush approved of Abbas's appointment, and the Quartet unveiled its plan, called the Roadmap for Peace.

The ultimate goal of the Roadmap for Peace is the creation of a Palestinian state by 2005. The plan is performance-based, which means that its success depends on how well each side follows through on its promises. It first calls for an end to violence between Israel and the Palestinians. In its second phase, it calls for the creation of a separate Palestinian state with temporary borders. In its final phase, Israel and the Palestinians would finalize the borders of the Palestinian state. But navigators of the map have already lost direction. Prime Minister Abbas resigned in September 2003 over issues of controlling PLO security forces. Violence erupted in Israel, and Sharon called on the military to resume assassinations of Hamas leaders. Arafat nominated Ahmed Qurei to replace Abbas. Qurei accepted on condition that all parties work together and guarantee adherence to the Roadmap for Peace. Sharon has pledged to continue the peace process.

Will It Ever End?

It's a lovely summer day in the city of Tel Aviv. The sun glints off cars in a crowded marketplace. A man stands alone amid the crowd. Several people glance at him suspiciously. His long coat looks out of place in this hot weather. The man in the coat looks up as an Israeli police officer approaches. He slips his hand in his coat. The next moment, an explosion shatters the blue sky, sending dust and glass into the air. Within minutes, paramedics arrive to help the victims of this latest suicide bombing.

Decades of fighting have taken a heavy toll. Many names and faces have changed in the long search for peace. Rabin is dead from a sniper's bullet. George Schultz and James Baker have moved on, passing the diplomatic torch to U.S. secretary of state Colin Powell. Two Bush administrations have tried their hand at peace negotiations. Throughout the years, the Israeli-Palestinian conflict has become a political issue. However, the first and second intifadas are proof that politics can only go so far. A peace treaty means nothing if it doesn't have the support of the people.

Even though the past is disheartening, there is hope for the future. Many peace organizations have turned their attention to the next generation. They are bringing Israeli and Palestinian children together to show them that they are the same beneath the surface. Perhaps these children will be the ones to do what their parents couldn't—live side by side in peace.

GLOSSARY

autonomy Self-government or the right of self-government; independence.

coalition An alliance, especially a temporary one, of people, factions, parties, or nations.

curfew A regulation requiring people to leave the streets or be at home at a certain hour.

dissenter One who withholds assent or approval.

exile Enforced removal from one's native country.

extremist One who advocates or resorts to measures beyond the norm, especially in politics.

intifada Arabic for "shaking off"; a term used for staging an uprising.

martyr One who chooses to suffer death in order to further a belief, cause, principle, or religious faith.

peace treaty A formal agreement between two or more countries promising that the countries will not wage war against each other.

renounce To formally give up or reject.

terrorism The unlawful use of force or the threat of force against people or property, often for ideological or political reasons.

Zionism An international movement created in the 1890s, originally committed to the establishment of a Jewish national homeland in Palestine. Since 1948, it has been committed to the support, defense, and preservation of the State of Israel.

Amnesty International
322 Eighth Avenue
New York, NY 10001
(212) 807-8400
Web site: http://www.amnestyusa.org

Council on American-Islamic Relations (CAIR)
453 New Jersey Avenue SE
Washington, DC 20003
(202) 488-8787
Web site: http://www.cair-net.org

Human Rights Watch (HRW)
350 Fifth Avenue, 34th Floor
New York, NY 10118-3299
(212) 290-4700
Web site: http://www.hrw.org

United States Department of State
2201 C Street NW
Washington, DC 20520
(202) 647-4000
Web site: http://www.state.gov

Web Sites

Due to the changing nature of Internet links, the Rosen Publishing Group, Inc., has developed an online list of Web sites related to the subject of this book. This site is updated regularly. Please use this link to access the list:

http://www.rosenlinks.com/wcme/infi

FOR FURTHER READING

Carew-Miller, Anna. *The Palestinians*. Philadelphia: Mason Crest Publishers, 2003.

Corona, Laurel. *Israel*. San Diego: Lucent Books, 2002.

Downing, David. *Yasser Arafat*. Chicago: Heinemann Library, 2002.

Gottfried, Ted. *The Israelis and Palestinians: Small Steps to Peace*. Brookfield, CT: Millbrook Press, 2000.

Greenberg, Keith. *The Middle East: Struggle for a Mideast Homeland*. Woodbridge, CT: Blackbirch Marketing, 1996.

Ojeda, Auriana, ed. *The Middle East*. San Diego: Greenhaven Press, 2003.

Sha'Ban, Mervet Akram, et al. *If You Could Be My Friend: Letters of Mervet Akram Sha'Ban and Galit Fink*. New York: Orchard Books, 1998.

Wagner, Heather Lehr. *Israel and the Arab World*. Philadelphia: Chelsea House Publications, 2002.

"Al-Aqsa Mosque." Noble Sanctuary Online Guide. Retrieved March 2003 (http://www.noblesanctuary.com/ AQSAMosque.html).

"Ariel Sharon." Jewish Virtual Library. Retrieved March 2003 (http://www.usisrael.org/jsource/biography/ sharon.html).

"Attacks Since Start of Al-Aqsa Intifada: A CNN Timeline." CNN.com. Retrieved May 2003 (http://www.cnn. com/2002/WORLD/meast/06/20/terror.attacks. chronology/).

Baer, Shaiya. Interview with the author. February 18, 2003.

Bard, Mitchell. *The Complete Idiot's Guide to Middle East Conflict*. Indianapolis: Macmillan, 1999.

Bennis, Phyllis, et al. "MERIP Primer on the Uprising in Palestine." The Middle East Research and Information Project. Retrieved May 2003 (http://www.merip.org/ new_uprising_primer/primer_all_text.html).

Cohn-Sherbok, Dan, and Dawoud El-Alami. *The Palestine-Israeli Conflict: A Beginner's Guide*. Oxford, England: Oneworld Publications Ltd., 2001.

"The Cycle of Violence." PBS Online. Retrieved May 2003 (http://www.pbs.org/wgbh/pages/frontline/shows/ holy/cron/).

Frankel, Glenn. *Beyond the Promised Land: Jews and Arabs on the Hard Road to a New Israel*. New York: Simon and Schuster, 1994.

Hunter, Robert F. *The Palestinian Uprising: A War by Other Means*. Berkeley, CA: University of California Press, 1991.

"Israel and the Occupied Territories: An Ongoing Human Rights Crisis." Amnesty International. Retrieved May 2003 (http://web.amnesty.org/pages/iot_home).

"Israel Defense Forces (IDF)—An Introduction." Jewish Virtual Library. Retrieved April 2003 (http://www. us-israel.org/jsource/Society_&_Culture/IDF.html).

"Israel Makes Partial Withdrawal—Rewarded with Terror." Leyden Communications. Retrieved May 2003 (http://www.israelpr.com/israelterrorbus.html).

Kimmerling, Baruch, and Joel S. Migdal. *Palestinians: The Making of a People*. New York: Macmillan, 1993.

Montell, Jessica. "Operation Defensive Shield: The Propaganda War and the Reality." *Tikkun*. July/August 2002. Retrieved May 2003 (http://www.tikkun.org/magazine/index.cfm/action/ tikkun/issue/tik0207/article/020711a.html).

Ramadan, Saud Abu. "Oslo Accord Architect Named Palestinian PM." *Washington Times*, March 8, 2003. Retrieved May 2003 (http://www.washtimes.com/ upi-breaking/20030308-112313-4608r.htm).

Schiff, Ze'ev, and Ehud Ya'ari. *Intifada: The Palestinian Uprising—Israel's Third Front*. New York: Simon and Schuster, 1989.

Stein, Yael. "Events on the Temple Mount: 29 September 2000." B'Tselem, The Israel Information Center for Human Rights in the Occupied Territories. Retrieved April 2003 (http://www.btselem.org).

"Text of Proposed 'Road Map.'" The Electronic Intifada. Retrieved May 2003 (http://electronicintifada.net/ v2/article1410.shtml).

"Units." Israel Defense Forces. Retrieved March 2003 (http://www.idf.il/english/organization/ organization.stm).

"Yasser Arafat." ABC News.com. Retrieved March 2003 (http://abcnews.go.com/reference/bios/arafat.html).

"Yasser Arafat—Biography." Nobel e-Museum, February 21, 2003. Retrieved March 2003 (http://www.nobel.se/ peace/laureates/1994/arafat-bio.html).

"Yitzhak Rabin—Biography." Nobel e-Museum, June 4, 2002. Retrieved May 2003 (http://www.nobel.se/ peace/laureates/1994/rabin-bio.html).

"Yitzhak Rabin 1922–1995." Israel Ministry of Foreign Affairs. Retrieved May 2003 (http://www.israel.org/ mfa/go.asp?MFAH00ga0).

"Yitzhak Shamir." Jewish Virtual Library. Retrieved March 2003 (http://www.us-israel.org/jsource/biography/ shamir.html).

INDEX

About the Author

Katherine Wingate lives with her husband and daughter in Tennessee.

Photo Credits

Cover, pp. 46–47, 51 © Corbis; pp. 1, 3, 4–5, 12–13, 14, 17, 18, 20–21, 25, 28, 44, 48 © Peter Turnley/ Corbis; pp. 6–7, 10 © Max Nash/AP/World Wide Photos; p. 27 © Bernard Bisson/Corbis; p. 30–31 © Bettmann/ Corbis; p. 32 © Robert Patrick/Corbis; p. 35 © Ricki Rosen/Corbis; p. 36 © AP/World Wide Photos; pp. 38–39, 42, 52 © Reuters New Media Inc./Corbis; p. 41 © David Rubinger/Corbis.

Designer: Nelson Sá; **Editor:** Mark Beyer;
Photo Researcher: Nelson Sá